Practical
Barbecue

p^3

This is a P³ Publishing Book
This edition published in 2002

P³ Publishing
Queen Street House
4 Queen Street
Bath BA1 1HE

ISBN: 0-75259-367-6

Printed in China

NOTE

Cup measurements in this book are for American cups.
This book also uses imperial and metric measurements. Follow the same units
of measurement throughout; do not mix imperial and metric.
All spoon measurements are level: teaspoons are assumed to be 5 ml, and
tablespoons are assumed to be 15 ml. Unless otherwise stated,
milk is assumed to be whole milk, eggs and individual vegetables such as potatoes
are medium, and pepper is freshly ground black pepper.

The nutritional information provided for each recipe is per serving or per person.
Optional ingredients, variations, or serving suggestions have
not been included in the calculations. The times given for each recipe are an approximate
guide only because the preparation times may differ according to the techniques used by
different people and the cooking times may vary as a result of the type of oven used.

Recipes using raw or very lightly cooked eggs should be
avoided by infants, the elderly, pregnant women, convalescents,
and anyone suffering from an illness.

Contents

Introduction

What is it that makes a meal cooked outdoors over burning coals so appetizing? Perhaps it is the fresh air or the tantalizing aroma or the sound of food sizzling on the cooking rack. Whatever it is, there is no doubt that barbecues and outdoor grills are becoming more and more popular. This is hardly surprising when you see just how many marvelous dishes can be cooked over charcoal. This book alone contains 27 recipes, leaving you with no shortage of inspiration. Gone are the days when sausages and burgers were the staple of every barbecue party, although traditionalists will find recipes here for making fabulous burgers and for tangy sauces to serve with the sausages. But why not try fish, which cooks to perfection on the barbecue grill and is healthy too? There are also dozens of tasty marinades and bastes for meat lovers, as well as vegetarian dishes, salads, and side dishes. You can even cook a dessert on the barbecue.

Which barbecue grill?

You do not need a large, sophisticated barbecue grill to produce mouthwatering food, although once you have tried some of these recipes you might want to invest in something larger.

Essentially, barbecue grills are an open fire with a rack set over the hot coals, on which the food is cooked. You can improvise a makeshift barbecue grill with nothing more complicated than a few house bricks and an old oven rack. Chicken wire and baking racks can also be used for cooking. Purpose-made barbecues or outdoor grills are, however, available in all shapes and sizes, from small disposable trays to large wagon models, powered by bottled gas.

As the names suggest, portable and semiportable barbecues tend to be small. Some types have a stand or folding legs; others have fixed legs. If you have a small model and are cooking for large numbers of people, cook the food in rotation so that guests can begin on the first batch while the second batch is cooking. Most brazier barbecues, which stand on long legs and have a windshield, are light and portable. On some models the height of the rack can be varied, and some types incorporate rotisseries.

Covered barbecues are essential if you want to cook whole joints of meat. The lid completely covers the grill, increasing the temperature at which food cooks and acting, in effect, like an oven. The temperature is controlled by air vents. When used without the cover, these barbecue grills are treated like traditional barbecue grills.

Wagon barbecues or outdoor grills are larger and more sophisticated. They have wheels and often incorporate a handy tabletop.

Electric or gas barbecue grills heat volcanic lava coals. The flavor is still good, because the flavor of barbecued food comes from the aromas of fat and juices burning on the coals rather than just from the fuel itself.

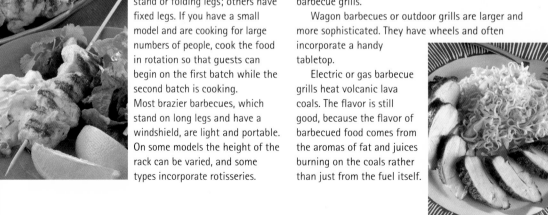

Equipment

Apart from the barbecue grill itself, you do not need any special equipment, but do arm yourself with a pair of oven mitts. Long-handled tools can be useful, as well as being safer and more convenient to use. They are not expensive, and if you cook on a barbecue regularly it is a good idea to invest in a set. Specially shaped racks for burgers, sausages, and fish are useful but not essential.

You will need a set of skewers if you want to cook kabobs. Metal skewers should be flat to stop the food slipping around as it cooks. Remember that metal skewers get very hot, so wear oven mitts or use tongs to turn them. Wooden skewers are much cheaper than metal skewers but are not always very long-lasting. Always soak wooden skewers in cold water for at least 30 minutes before use to help prevent them from burning on the barbecue grill and then cover the exposed ends with pieces of aluminum foil. A water spray is useful for cooling down coals or dampening down flare-ups.

Lighting the barbecue grill

Charcoal is the most popular fuel although you can use wood. Charcoal is available as lump wood, which is irregular in shape and size but easy to light, or as briquettes, which burn for longer and with a more uniform heat but are harder to light.

Light the grill at least an hour before you want to start cooking. Stack the coals in the pan and use specially designed solid or liquid lighter fuels to help set the charcoal alight. Do not use household fire lighters because these will taint the food. Never use kerosene or gasoline to light a barbecue grill—it is very dangerous if used incorrectly.

The barbecue grill is ready to use when the flames have died down and the coals are covered with a white ash. When the coals are ready, spread them out into a uniform layer.

Preparing to cook

Before you begin to cook, oil the rack so that the food does not stick to it. Do this away from the barbecue or the oil will flare up as it drips onto the coals. For most dishes, position the rack about 3 inches/7.5 cm above the coals. Raise the rack if you want to slow down the cooking. If you cannot adjust the height of the rack, slow down cooking by spreading out the coals or moving the food to the edges where the heat will be less intense.

If your barbecue grill has air vents, use them to control the temperature—open the vents for more heat, close them to reduce the temperature.

It is very difficult to give exact times for cooking on a barbecue, so use the times given in the recipes in this book as a guide only. Always test the food to make sure that it is cooked thoroughly before serving.

Lamb on Rosemary Skewers

Wild rosemary scents the air all over the Mediterranean—here, sprigs are used as skewers for succulent lamb cubes with Turkish flavorings.

NUTRITIONAL INFORMATION

Calories	286	Sugars	.........5g
Protein	........27g	Fat	..........16g
Carbohydrate	....7g	Saturates	.......6g

10 mins, plus 4 hrs marinating   10–12 mins

MAKES 4

I N G R E D I E N T S

1 lb 2 oz/500 g boneless leg of lamb

4 long, thick branches fresh rosemary

1 large or 2 small red bell peppers

12 large garlic cloves, peeled

olive oil, for cooking

Spiced Pilau with Saffron (see page 30), to serve

M A R I N A D E

2 tbsp olive oil

2 tbsp dry white wine

½ tsp ground cumin

1 sprig fresh oregano, chopped

1 Cut the lamb into 2-inch/5-cm cubes. Mix the marinade ingredients in a bowl. Add the lamb, stir well to coat and let marinate for 4–12 hours.

2 An hour before cooking, put the rosemary in a bowl of cold water and let soak.

3 Slice the tops off the bell peppers, cut into fourths, and remove the cores and seeds. Cut the quarters into 2 inch/ 5 cm pieces.

4 Bring a small pan of water to a boil. Add the pepper pieces and garlic and blanch for 1 minute. Drain and refresh under cold water. Pat dry and set aside.

5 Drain the rosemary and pat dry. Remove the needles from the first 1½ inches/4 cm of the branches to make handles for turning while grilling.

6 Thread pieces of lamb, garlic, and pepper onto the herb skewers: the meat should be tender enough to push a sprig through it. If not, use a metal skewer to poke a hole through each cube.

7 Lightly oil the barbecue grill rack. Put the skewers on the rack, 5 inches/ 12.5 cm away from the heat source, and cook for 10–12 minutes, brushing with leftover marinade or oil and turning, until the meat is cooked. Serve with the pilau.

Boozy Beef Steaks

A simple marinade gives plain grilled steaks a fabulous flavor in return for very little effort in the kitchen.

NUTRITIONAL INFORMATION

Calories 371	Sugars 5g
Protein 48g	Fat 14g
Carbohydrate 6g	Saturates 6g

2 mins, plus 2 hrs marinating   15–25 mins

SERVES 4

I N G R E D I E N T S

4 beef steaks

4 tbsp whiskey or brandy

2 tbsp soy sauce

1 tbsp dark brown sugar

pepper

fresh sprigs of parsley, to garnish

T O   S E R V E

garlic bread

slices of tomato

1 Make a few cuts in the edge of the fat on each steak. This will stop the meat curling as it cooks.

2 Place the beef steaks in a shallow, nonmetallic dish.

3 Combine the whiskey or brandy, soy sauce, and sugar in a bowl. Add pepper to taste, and stir until the sugar dissolves. Pour the mixture over the steak. Cover and let marinate for at least 2 hours.

4 Grill the beef steaks over hot coals, searing the meat over the hottest part of the barbecue grill for about 2 minutes on each side.

5 Move the beef to an area with slightly less intense heat and cook for another 4–10 minutes on each side, depending on how well done you like your steaks. Test the meat is cooked by inserting the tip of a knife—the juices will run from red when the meat is still rare, to clear as it becomes well cooked.

6 Lightly grill the slices of tomato for 1–2 minutes.

7 Transfer the meat and the tomatoes to warm plates. Garnish with sprigs of parsley and serve with garlic bread.

Beef, Tomato & Olive Kabobs

These kabobs have a Mediterranean flavor. The sweetness of the tomatoes and the sharpness of the olives makes them irresistible.

NUTRITIONAL INFORMATION

Calories	166	Sugars	.........1g
Protein	........12g	Fat	..........12g
Carbohydrate	....1g	Saturates	......3g

🔺 5 mins   🕐 10–17 mins

SERVES 4

I N G R E D I E N T S

1 lb/450 g rump or sirloin steak

16 cherry tomatoes

16 large green olives, pitted

salt and freshly ground black pepper

focaccia bread, to serve

B A S T E

4 tbsp olive oil

1 tbsp sherry vinegar

1 garlic clove, crushed

F R E S H   T O M A T O   R E L I S H

1 tbsp olive oil

½ red onion, finely chopped

1 garlic clove, chopped

6 plum tomatoes, skinned, seeded, and chopped

2 green olives, pitted and sliced

1 tbsp chopped fresh parsley

1 tbsp lemon juice

1 Trim any fat from the meat and cut into about 24 even-size pieces.

2 Thread the meat onto 8 skewers, alternating it with cherry tomatoes and the pitted whole olives.

3 To make the baste, combine the oil, vinegar, garlic, and salt and pepper to taste in a bowl.

4 To make the fresh tomato relish, heat the oil in a small pan and cook the onion and garlic for 3–4 minutes, until softened. Add the tomatoes and sliced olives and cook for 2–3 minutes until the tomatoes are softened slightly. Stir in the parsley and lemon juice, and season with salt and pepper to taste. Set aside and keep warm or let chill.

5 Grill the skewers on an oiled rack over hot coals for 5–10 minutes, basting and turning frequently. Serve with the tomato relish and slices of focaccia.

Beef Satay

Satay recipes vary throughout the Far East, but these little beef skewers are a classic version of the traditional dish.

NUTRITIONAL INFORMATION

Calories	489	Sugars	........14g
Protein	........38g	Fat	..........31g
Carbohydrate	...17g	Saturates	.......8g

5 mins, plus 2 hrs marinating   3–5 mins

SERVES 4

I N G R E D I E N T S

1 lb 2 oz/500 g beef tenderloin

2 garlic cloves, crushed

1½ tsp finely grated fresh gingerroot

1 tbsp light brown sugar

1 tbsp dark soy sauce

1 tbsp lime juice

2 tsp sesame oil

1 tsp ground coriander

1 tsp turmeric

½ tsp chili powder

chopped cucumber and red bell pepper, to serve

P E A N U T   S A U C E

1¼ cups coconut milk

8 tbsp crunchy peanut butter

½ small onion, grated

2 tsp light brown sugar

½ tsp chili powder

1 tbsp dark soy sauce

1 Cut the beef into ½-inch/1-cm cubes and place in a large bowl.

2 Add the crushed garlic, grated ginger, sugar, soy sauce, lime juice, sesame oil, ground coriander, turmeric, and chili powder. Mix together well to coat the pieces of meat evenly. Cover and let marinate in the refrigerator for at least 2 hours, or overnight.

3 For the peanut sauce, place all the ingredients in a pan and stir over medium heat until boiling. Remove from the heat and keep warm.

4 If using wooden skewers, soak for 20 minutes. Thread with the beef. Cook on a barbecue grill or under a preheated broiler for 3–5 minutes, turning often. Serve with the sauce, cucumber, and bell pepper.

Thai-Style Burgers

If your family likes to eat burgers, try these—they have a much more interesting flavor than conventional hamburgers.

NUTRITIONAL INFORMATION

Calories	358	Sugars	.........1g
Protein	........23g	Fat	..........29g
Carbohydrate	....2g	Saturates	.......5g

 5–10 mins   🕐 12–16 mins

SERVES 4

I N G R E D I E N T S

1 small lemongrass stem

1 small red chile, seeded

2 garlic cloves, peeled

2 scallions

7 oz/200 g closed-cup mushrooms

14 oz/400 g ground pork

1 tbsp Thai fish sauce

3 tbsp chopped fresh cilantro

sunflower oil, for cooking

2 tbsp mayonnaise

1 tbsp lime juice

salt and pepper

TO SERVE

4 sesame hamburger buns

shredded napa cabbage

2 In a large bowl, mix the chopped mushroom paste with the ground pork, Thai fish sauce, and cilantro. Season well with salt and pepper, then divide the mixture into 4 equal portions. Using lightly floured hands, form the pieces into flat burger shapes.

3 Brush the burgers with oil and cook over medium-hot coals, or heat some oil in a skillet and cook over medium heat, for 6–8 minutes.

4 Meanwhile, mix the mayonnaise with the lime juice. Split the hamburger buns and spread the lime-flavored mayonnaise on the cut surfaces. Add a few shredded napa cabbage leaves, top with a burger, and sandwich together. Serve immediately, while still hot.

1 Place the lemongrass, chile, garlic, and scallions in a food processor and blend to a smooth paste. Add the mushrooms and chop very finely.

Bacon & Scallop Skewers

Wrapping bacon around the scallops helps to protect the delicate flesh from the intense heat and lets them cook without becoming tough.

NUTRITIONAL INFORMATION

Calories 271	Sugars 6g		
Protein 17g	Fat 20g		
Carbohydrate 7g	Saturates 5g		

10 mins, plus 1–2 hrs marinating

5 mins

MAKES 4

I N G R E D I E N T S

grated zest and juice of ½ lemon

4 tbsp sunflower oil

½ tsp dried dill

12 scallops

1 red bell pepper

1 green bell pepper

1 yellow bell pepper

6 strips smoked lean bacon

1 Mix together the lemon zest and juice, oil, and dill in a nonmetallic dish. Add the scallops and mix thoroughly to coat. Let marinate for 1–2 hours.

2 Cut the red, green, and yellow bell peppers in half and seed them. Cut the bell pepper halves into 1-inch/2.5-cm pieces and then set aside until required.

3 Remove the rind from the bacon strips. Stretch the strips with the back of a knife, then cut each strip in half.

4 Remove the scallops from the marinade, reserving any excess marinade. Wrap a piece of bacon firmly around each scallop.

5 Thread the bacon-wrapped scallops onto skewers, alternating with the bell pepper pieces.

6 Grill the bacon and scallop skewers over hot coals for about 5 minutes, basting frequently with the lemon and the oil marinade.

7 Transfer the skewers to serving plates and serve immediately.

VARIATION

Peel 4–8 raw shrimp and add them to the marinade with the scallops. Thread them onto the skewers alternately with the scallops and bell peppers.

Tangy Pork Tenderloin

Grilled until tender in a parcel of foil, these cuts of tasty pork are served with a tangy orange sauce.

NUTRITIONAL INFORMATION

Calories . . . . . . .230g   Sugars 16g
Protein . . . . .19g   Fat 9g
Carbohydrate . . .20g   Saturates 3g

🄸 🄸

🥄 10 mins   ⏲ 55 mins

SERVES 4

I N G R E D I E N T S

14 oz/400 g lean pork tenderloin

3 tbsp orange marmalade

grated zest and juice of 1 orange

1 tbsp white wine vinegar

dash of Tabasco sauce

salt and pepper

S A U C E

1 tbsp olive oil

1 small onion, chopped

1 small, green bell pepper, seeded and thinly sliced

1 tbsp cornstarch

⅔ cup orange juice

T O S E R V E

cooked rice

salad greens

1 Place a large piece of double thickness foil in a shallow dish. Put the pork tenderloin in the center of the foil and season to taste.

2 Heat the marmalade, orange zest and juice, vinegar, and Tabasco sauce in a small pan, stirring, until the marmalade melts and the ingredients combine. Pour the mixture over the pork and wrap the meat in the foil. Seal the parcel well so that the juices cannot run out. Place over hot coals and grill for about 25 minutes, turning the parcel occasionally.

3 For the sauce, heat the oil in a pan and cook the onion for 2–3 minutes. Add the bell pepper and cook for 3–4 minutes.

4 Remove the pork from the foil and place onto the rack. Pour the juices into the pan with the sauce.

5 Continue grilling the pork for another 10–20 minutes, turning, until cooked through and golden.

6 In a bowl, mix the cornstarch into a paste with a little orange juice. Add to the sauce with the remaining cooking juices. Cook, stirring, until it thickens. Slice the pork, spoon over the sauce, and serve with rice and salad greens.

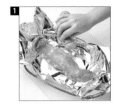

Tequila Chicken Wings

Tequila tenderizes these tasty chicken wings. Serve them accompanied by corn tortillas, refried beans, salsa, and lots of chilled beer.

NUTRITIONAL INFORMATION

Calories	489	Sugars	.........8g
Protein	........41g	Fat	..........30g
Carbohydrate	....11g	Saturates	.......7g

	5 mins, plus 3 hrs marinating	15–20 mins

SERVES 4

INGREDIENTS

2 lb/900 g chicken wings

11 garlic cloves, finely chopped

juice of 2 limes

juice of 1 orange

2 tbsp tequila

1 tbsp mild chili powder

2 dried chipotle chilies, reconstituted and pureed

2 tbsp vegetable oil

1 tsp sugar

¼ tsp ground allspice

pinch of ground cinnamon

pinch of ground cumin

pinch of dried oregano

1 Cut the chicken wings into two pieces at the joint and place them in a nonmetallic bowl.

2 In a separate bowl, combine the remaining ingredients thoroughly. Pour over the chicken wings, toss well to coat, cover, then place in the refrigerator to marinate for at least 3 hours, or preferably overnight.

3 Grill the chicken wings over hot coals or in a ridged grill pan for about 15–20 minutes, or until the wings are crisply browned, turning occasionally. To test whether the chicken is cooked, pierce a thick part with a skewer—the juices should run clear. Serve immediately.

COOK'S TIP

Made from the agave plant, tequila is Mexico's famous alcoholic drink.

Indian Charred Chicken

An Indian-influenced dish that is delicious served with nan bread and a cucumber raita.

NUTRITIONAL INFORMATION

Calories . . . . . . .228 Sugars 12g
Protein . . . . .28g Fat 8g
Carbohydrate . . .12g Saturates 2g

🧊 20 mins   🕐 10 mins

SERVES 4

I N G R E D I E N T S

4 chicken breasts, skinned and boned

2 tbsp curry paste

1 tbsp sunflower oil, plus extra for cooking

1 tbsp brown sugar

1 tsp ground ginger

½ tsp ground cumin

T O   S E R V E

nan bread

salad greens

C U C U M B E R   R A I T A

¼ cucumber

salt

⅔ cup lowfat unsweetened yogurt

¼ tsp chili powder

1 Place the chicken breasts between 2 sheets of baking parchment or plastic wrap. Pound them with the flat side of a meat mallet or rolling pin to flatten them.

2 Mix together the curry paste, oil, sugar, ginger, and cumin in a small bowl. Spread the mixture over both sides of the chicken and set aside until required.

3 To make the raita, peel the cucumber and scoop out the seeds with a spoon. Grate the cucumber flesh, sprinkle with

salt, place in a strainer, and let stand for 10 minutes. Rinse off the salt and squeeze out any remaining moisture by pressing the cucumber with the bottom of a glass or the back of a spoon.

4 In a small bowl, mix the grated cucumber with the unsweetened yogurt and stir in the chili powder. Let chill until required.

5 Transfer the chicken pieces to an oiled rack and grill over hot coals for 10 minutes, turning once.

6 Warm the nan bread at the side of the barbecue grill.

7 Serve the chicken with the nan bread and cucumber raita, accompanied by fresh salad greens.

Lemon Chicken Skewers

A tangy lemon yogurt flavored with cilantro is served with these tasty marinated chicken kabobs.

NUTRITIONAL INFORMATION

Calories	187	Sugars	.........6g
Protein	........34g	Fat	...........3g
Carbohydrate	....6g	Saturates	.......1g

 5 mins, plus 2 hrs chilling   15 mins

SERVES 4

INGREDIENTS

4 chicken breasts, skinned and boned

1 tsp ground coriander

2 tsp lemon juice

1¼ cups unsweetened yogurt

1 lemon

2 tbsp chopped fresh cilantro

oil, for brushing

salt and pepper

sprigs of fresh cilantro, to garnish

TO SERVE

lemon wedges

salad greens

1 Cut the chicken into 1-inch/2.5-cm pieces and place them in a shallow, nonmetallic dish.

2 Add the ground coriander, lemon juice, 4 tablespoons of the yogurt, and salt and pepper to taste. Mix together until thoroughly combined. Cover with plastic wrap and chill for at least 2 hours, preferably overnight.

3 To make the lemon yogurt, peel and finely chop the lemon, discarding any pips. In a bowl, stir the lemon into the remaining yogurt along with the chopped cilantro. Chill until required.

4 Thread the chicken pieces onto skewers. Brush the rack with oil, baste the skewers with it, then place them on the rack. Grill over hot coals for about 15 minutes, basting.

5 Transfer the cooked chicken kabobs to warm serving plates and garnish with sprigs of fresh cilantro, lemon wedges, and fresh salad greens. Serve the chicken with the lemon yogurt.

VARIATION

These kabobs are delicious served on a bed of blanched spinach that has been seasoned with salt, pepper, and nutmeg.

Turkey with Cheese Pockets

Wrapping bacon around the turkey adds extra flavor, and helps to keep the cheese enclosed in the pocket.

NUTRITIONAL INFORMATION

Calories 518	Sugars 0g	
Protein 66g	Fat 28g	
Carbohydrate 0g	Saturates 9g	

🕐 10 mins   ⏱ 20 mins

SERVES 4

I N G R E D I E N T S

4 turkey breast pieces, about
   8 oz/225 g each

4 portions of fullfat cheese (such as Bel
   Paese), ½ oz/15 g each

4 fresh sage leaves or ½ tsp dried sage

8 strips rindless lean bacon

4 tbsp olive oil

2 tbsp lemon juice

salt and pepper

TO SERVE

garlic bread

salad greens

cherry tomatoes

1 Carefully cut a pocket into the side of each turkey breast. Open out each breast a little and season inside with salt and pepper to taste.

2 Place a portion of cheese into each pocket. Tuck a sage leaf into each pocket, or sprinkle with a little dried sage.

3 Stretch out the bacon with the back of a knife. Wrap 2 strips around each turkey breast, covering the pocket.

4 Mix together the oil and lemon juice in a small bowl.

5 Grill the turkey over medium-hot coals, 10 minutes each side, basting frequently with the lemon mixture.

6 Place the garlic bread at the side of the barbecue grill and toast lightly.

7 Transfer the turkey to warm serving plates. Serve with the toasted garlic bread, salad greens, and cherry tomatoes.

VARIATION

You can vary the cheese you use to stuff the turkey—try grated mozzarella or slices of Brie or Camembert. Also try 1 teaspoon of redcurrant jelly or cranberry sauce in each pocket instead of the sage.

Filipino Chicken

Tomato catsup is a very popular ingredient in Asian dishes because it imparts a zingy sweet-sour flavor.

NUTRITIONAL INFORMATION

Calories ....197 Sugars 7g
Protein ....28g Fat 4g
Carbohydrate ....8g Saturates 1g

10 mins, plus 2½ hrs marinating

20 mins

SERVES 4

INGREDIENTS

1¾ cups canned lemonade or lime-and-lemonade

2 tbsp gin

4 tbsp tomato catsup

2 tsp garlic salt

2 tsp Worcestershire sauce

4 lean chicken suprêmes or breast fillets

salt and pepper

TO SERVE

cooked thread egg noodles

1 red chile, finely chopped

2 scallions, sliced

1 Combine the lemonade or lime-and-lemonade, gin, tomato catsup, garlic salt, Worcestershire sauce, and seasoning in a large, nonporous dish.

2 Put the chicken pieces into the dish and make sure that the marinade covers them completely.

3 Let the meat marinate in the refrigerator for 2 hours. Remove from the refrigerator and let stand, covered, at room temperature for 30 minutes.

4 Place the chicken pieces over a medium-hot barbecue grill and cook for 20 minutes, turning once halfway through the cooking time.

5 Remove the cooked meat from the barbecue grill. Let rest for 3–4 minutes before serving.

6 Serve with egg noodles tossed with chopped red chile and sliced scallions.

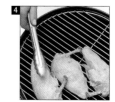

Duck with Pineapple Salsa

A salsa is a cross between a sauce and a relish. Salsas are easy to prepare and will liven up all kinds of simple grilled meats.

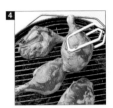

NUTRITIONAL INFORMATION

Calories	668	Sugars	........16g
Protein	.....41g	Fat	.........35g
Carbohydrate	...78g	Saturates	......15g

 5 mins, plus 1 hr marinating   40–45 mins

SERVES 2

I N G R E D I E N T S

2 tbsp Dijon mustard

1 tsp paprika

½ tsp ground ginger

½ tsp ground nutmeg

2 tbsp dark brown sugar

2 duckling halves

salad greens, to serve

PINEAPPLE SALSA

8 oz/225 g canned pineapple in natural juice

2 tbsp dark brown sugar

1 small red onion, finely chopped

1 red chile, seeded and chopped

1 To make the salsa, drain the canned pineapple, reserving 2 tablespoons of the juice. Finely chop the pineapple flesh.

2 Place the pineapple, reserved juice, sugar, onion, and chile in a bowl and mix well. Let stand for at least 1 hour for the flavors to develop fully.

3 Meanwhile, mix together the mustard, paprika, ginger, nutmeg, and sugar in a bowl. Spread the mixture evenly over the skin of the duckling halves.

4 Grill the duckling, skin-side up, over hot coals for about 30 minutes. Turn the duckling over and continue grilling for 10–15 minutes, or until the duckling is cooked through.

5 Serve with fresh salad greens and the pineapple salsa.

COOK'S TIP
Place the duckling on foil on a cookie sheet to protect the delicate flesh on the barbecue grill.

Grilled Scallops

These marinated scallops are grilled and then served with couscous studded with colorful vegetables and herbs.

NUTRITIONAL INFORMATION

Calories 401	Sugars 3g
Protein 20g	Fat 21g
Carbohydrate . . .34g	Saturates 3g

40 mins, plus 2 hrs marinating   12–13 mins

SERVES 4

INGREDIENTS

16 large scallops

3 tbsp olive oil

grated zest of 1 lime

2 tbsp chopped fresh basil

2 tbsp chopped fresh chives

1 garlic clove, finely chopped

black pepper

JEWELED COUSCOUS

8 oz/225 g couscous

½ yellow bell pepper, seeded and halved

½ red bell pepper, seeded and halved

4 tbsp extra-virgin olive oil

4 oz/115 g cucumber, chopped into
½-inch/1-cm pieces

3 scallions, finely chopped

1 tbsp lime juice

2 tbsp shredded fresh basil

salt and pepper

TO GARNISH

basil leaves

lime wedges

1 Clean and trim the scallops. Put into a nonmetallic dish. Mix together the olive oil, lime zest, basil, chives, garlic, and black pepper. Pour over the scallops and cover. Let marinate for 2 hours.

2 Cook the couscous according to the package instructions, omitting any butter recommended. Meanwhile, brush the bell pepper halves with olive oil and place under a preheated hot broiler for 5–6 minutes, turning once, until the skins are blackened and the flesh is tender. Put into a plastic bag to cool. Peel off the skins and chop the flesh into ½-inch/1-cm pieces. Add to the couscous with the remaining oil, and the cucumber, scallions, lime juice, and seasoning. Set aside.

3 Lift the scallops from the marinade and thread onto 4 skewers. Cook on a barbecue grill or preheated ridged grill pan for 1 minute on each side, until charred and firm but not quite cooked through. Remove from the heat and let rest for 2 minutes.

4 Stir the shredded basil into the couscous and divide between plates. Put a skewer on each, garnished with basil leaves and lime wedges.

Herb & Garlic Shrimp

A rich garlic and herb butter coats these shrimp kabobs, and cooking on a barbecue grill really brings out their flavor.

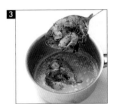

NUTRITIONAL INFORMATION

Calories 150	Sugars 0g
Protein 16g	Fat 9g
Carbohydrate 1g	Saturates 5g

5 mins, plus 30 mins marinating   7–12 mins

SERVES 4

I N G R E D I E N T S

12 oz/350 g raw shrimp, peeled

2 tbsp chopped fresh parsley

4 tbsp lemon juice

2 tbsp olive oil

5 tbsp butter

2 garlic cloves, chopped

salt and pepper

1 Place the prepared shrimp in a shallow, nonmetallic dish with the parsley, lemon juice, and salt and pepper to taste. Let the shrimp marinate in the herb mixture for at least 30 minutes.

2 Heat the oil and butter with the garlic in a small pan until the butter melts. Stir to mix thoroughly.

3 Use a slotted spoon to remove the shrimp from the marinade and add them to the pan containing the garlic butter. Stir the shrimp into the garlic butter until well coated, then thread them onto skewers.

4 Grill the kabobs over hot coals for 5–10 minutes, turning the skewers occasionally, until the shrimp turn pink and are cooked through. Brush the shrimp with the remaining garlic butter during the cooking time.

5 Transfer the herb and garlic shrimp kabobs to serving plates. Drizzle over any of the remaining garlic butter and serve at once.

VARIATION
If raw shrimp are unavailable, use cooked shrimp but reduce the cooking time. Small cooked shrimp can be prepared in foil parcels instead of on skewers. Marinate them in the garlic butter, wrap in foil, and cook for 5 minutes, shaking the parcels once or twice.

Mixed Seafood Brochettes

If your fish dealer sells halibut in steaks, you will probably need one large steak for this dish, cut into chunks.

NUTRITIONAL INFORMATION

Calories	455	Sugars	.......0.1g
Protein	........32g	Fat	..........20g
Carbohydrate	...39g	Saturates	.......9g

10 mins, plus 2 hrs marinating   20 mins

SERVES 4

I N G R E D I E N T S

8 oz/225 g skinless, boneless halibut fillet

8 oz/225 g skinless, boneless salmon fillet

8 scallops

8 large jumbo shrimp or langoustines

16 fresh bay leaves

1 lemon, cut into wedges

4 tbsp olive oil

grated zest of 1 lemon

4 tbsp chopped fresh mixed herbs such as thyme, parsley, chives, and basil

black pepper

L E M O N   B U T T E R   R I C E

6 oz/175 g long-grain rice

grated zest and juice of 1 lemon

4 tbsp butter

salt and pepper

T O   G A R N I S H

lemon wedges

sprigs of fresh dill

1 Chop the halibut and salmon fillets into 8 pieces each. Thread onto 8 skewers, alternating with the scallops, jumbo shrimp or langoustines, bay leaves, and lemon wedges. Put into a nonmetallic dish in a single layer.

2 Mix together the olive oil, lemon zest, mixed herbs, and black pepper. Pour the mixture over the fish. Cover and let marinate for 2 hours, turning once or twice.

3 For the lemon butter rice, bring a large pan of salted water to a boil and add the rice and lemon zest. Return to a boil and simmer for 7–8 minutes, until the rice is tender. Drain well and immediately stir in the lemon juice and butter. Season with salt and pepper to taste.

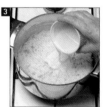

4 Meanwhile, lift the fish brochettes from their marinade and cook on a barbecue grill, under a preheated hot broiler, or in a preheated ridged grill pan for 8–10 minutes, turning regularly, until cooked through. Serve with lemon butter rice garnished with lemon wedges and dill.

Stuffed Mackerel

This is a simple variation of a difficult Middle-Eastern recipe, which involves removing the fish flesh and reserving and restuffing the skin.

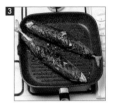

NUTRITIONAL INFORMATION

Calories	488	Sugars	........12g
Protein	........34g	Fat	..........34g
Carbohydrate	...12g	Saturates	.......6g

 5 mins   16 mins

SERVES 4

I N G R E D I E N T S

4 large mackerel, gutted and cleaned

1 tbsp olive oil

1 small onion, finely sliced

1 tsp ground cinnamon

½ tsp ground ginger

2 tbsp raisins

2 tbsp pine nuts, toasted

8 grape leaves in brine, drained

salt and pepper

VARIATION
This simple, easy-to-make pine nut stuffing works equally well with many other types of fish, including sea bass and red mullet.

1 Wash and dry the mackerel and set aside. Heat the oil in a small skillet and add the onion. Cook gently for 5 minutes, until softened. Add the ground cinnamon and ginger and cook for 30 seconds before adding the raisins, pine nuts, and seasoning. Remove from the heat and let cool.

2 Stuff each of the fish with a quarter of the onion and pine nut mixture.

Wrap each stuffed fish in 2 grape leaves, securing them with toothpicks.

3 Cook on a preheated barbecue grill or ridged grill pan for 5 minutes on each side, until the grape leaves have scorched and the fish is tender. Serve immediately.

Mediterranean Sardines

These tasty sardines will bring back memories of Mediterranean vacations. Serve them with crusty brown bread as a perfect appetizer.

NUTRITIONAL INFORMATION

Calories ....857 Sugars 0g
Protein ....88g Fat 56g
Carbohydrate ....0g Saturates 11g

15 mins, plus 30 mins marinating   6–8 mins

SERVES 4

INGREDIENTS

8–12 fresh sardines

8–12 sprigs of fresh thyme

3 tbsp lemon juice

4 tbsp olive oil

salt and pepper

TO GARNISH

lemon wedges

tomato slices

fresh herbs

1 Clean and gut the fish if this has not already been done by your fish dealer.

2 Remove the scales from the sardines by rubbing the back of a knife along the body from tail to head. Wash the sardines and pat dry with absorbent paper towels.

3 Tuck a sprig of fresh thyme into the body of each sardine.

4 Transfer the sardines to a large, nonmetallic dish and season with salt and pepper to taste.

5 In a separate bowl, beat together the lemon juice and oil and pour the mixture over the sardines. Let marinate in the refrigerator for about 30 minutes.

6 Remove the sardines from the marinade and place them in a hinged basket, if you have one, or on a rack. Grill the sardines over hot coals for 3–4 minutes on each side, basting frequently with any of the remaining marinade.

7 Serve the cooked sardines garnished with lemon wedges, tomato slices, and plenty of fresh herbs.

VARIATION

For a slightly different flavor and texture, give the sardines a crispy coating by tossing them in dried bread crumbs and basting them with a little olive oil.

Barbecued Monkfish

Monkfish is an ideal fish for cooking on a barbecue grill because of its firm flesh, which stays solid on the skewers as it cooks.

NUTRITIONAL INFORMATION

Calories 219	Sugars 0.1g	
Protein 28g	Fat 12g	
Carbohydrate 1g	Saturates 2g	

5 mins, plus 2 hrs marinating/ soaking   5–6 mins

SERVES 4

INGREDIENTS

4 tbsp olive oil

grated zest of 1 lime

2 tsp Thai fish sauce

2 garlic cloves, crushed

1 tsp grated fresh gingerroot

2 tbsp chopped fresh basil

1 lb 9 oz/700 g monkfish fillet, cut into chunks

2 limes, each cut into 6 wedges

salt and pepper

1 In a bowl, mix together the olive oil, lime zest, fish sauce, garlic, ginger, and basil. Season and set aside.

2 Wash the monkfish chunks and pat dry with paper towels. Add the chunks to the marinade and mix well. Let marinate for 2 hours, stirring occasionally.

3 If you are using bamboo skewers, soak them in cold water for 30 minutes. Then, lift the monkfish pieces from the marinade and thread them onto the skewers, alternating with the lime wedges.

4 Transfer the skewers, either to a barbecue or to a preheated ridged grill pan. Cook for 5–6 minutes, turning regularly, until the fish is tender. Serve immediately.

VARIATION

You could use any other white-fleshed fish for this recipe, but sprinkle the pieces with salt and stand for 2 hours to firm the flesh, before rinsing, drying, and then adding to the marinade.

Lemon Herrings

Cooking these fish in foil parcels gives them a marvelously moist texture. They make a perfect dinner party appetizer.

NUTRITIONAL INFORMATION

Calories	355	Sugars	.........0g
Protein	.........19g	Fat	...........31g
Carbohydrate	....0g	Saturates	......13g

 5 mins   🕐 15–20 mins

SERVES 4

I N G R E D I E N T S

4 herrings, gutted and scaled (if you prefer to scale your own fish, see step 2, page 23)

salt

4 bay leaves

1 lemon, sliced

4 tbsp unsalted butter

2 tbsp chopped fresh parsley

½ tsp lemon pepper

fresh crusty bread, to serve

1 Season the prepared herrings inside and out with freshly ground salt to taste.

2 Place a bay leaf inside the cavity of each fish.

3 Place 4 squares of foil on the counter and divide the lemon slices evenly among them. Place a fish on top of the lemon slices on each of the foil squares.

4 In a bowl, beat the butter until softened, then mix in the parsley and lemon pepper. Dot the flavored butter liberally all over the fish.

5 Wrap the fish tightly in the foil and grill over medium-hot coals for 15–20 minutes, or until the fish is cooked through—the flesh should be white in

color, and should feel firm to the touch (unwrap the foil to check, then wrap up the fish again).

6 Transfer the wrapped fish parcels to individual, warm serving plates.

7 Unwrap the foil parcels just before serving and serve the fish with fresh crusty bread to mop up the deliciously flavored cooking juices.

VARIATION

For an entrée, use trout instead of herring. Cook the trout for 20–30 minutes, until the flesh is opaque and firm to the touch.

Fragrant Tuna Steaks

Fresh tuna steaks are very meaty—they have a firm texture, yet the flesh is succulent. Steaks from the belly are best of all.

NUTRITIONAL INFORMATION

Calories	239	Sugars	.......0.1g
Protein	........42g	Fat	..........8g
Carbohydrate	...0.5g	Saturates	......2g

15 mins   15 mins

SERVES 4

I N G R E D I E N T S

4 tuna steaks, about 6 oz/175 g each

½ tsp finely grated lime zest

1 garlic clove, crushed

2 tsp olive oil

1 tsp ground cumin

1 tsp ground coriander

pepper

1 tbsp lime juice

sprigs of fresh cilantro, to garnish

TO SERVE

avocado relish (see Cook's Tip, below)

lime wedges

tomato wedges

COOK'S TIP

To make avocado relish, peel and chop a small, ripe avocado. Mix in 1 tablespoon of lime juice, 1 tablespoon of freshly chopped cilantro, 1 small, finely chopped red onion, and some chopped fresh mango or tomato. Season to taste.

1 Trim the skin from the tuna steaks, then rinse and pat dry on absorbent paper towels.

2 In a small bowl, mix together the lime zest, garlic, olive oil, cumin, ground coriander, and pepper to make a paste.

3 Spread the paste thinly on both sides of the tuna. Cook the tuna steaks for 5 minutes, turning once, on a foil-covered barbecue grill rack over hot coals, or in an oiled, ridged grill pan over high heat, in batches if necessary. Cook for another 4–5 minutes, drain on paper towels, and transfer to a serving plate.

4 Sprinkle the lime juice and sprigs of fresh cilantro over the cooked fish. Serve the tuna steaks with avocado relish (see Cook's Tip), and wedges of lime and tomato.

Vegetarian Sausages

These deliciously cheesy sausages will be a hit with vegetarians who have no need to feel left out when it comes to tasty grilled food.

NUTRITIONAL INFORMATION

Calories . . . . .213 Sugars 4g
Protein . . . . .8g Fat 12g
Carbohydrate . . .19g Saturates 4g

10 mins, plus 30 mins chilling   15–20 mins

MAKES 8

I N G R E D I E N T S

1 tbsp sunflower oil

1 small onion, finely chopped

½ cup finely chopped mushrooms

½ red bell pepper, seeded and finely chopped

14 oz/400 g canned cannellini beans, rinsed and drained

scant 2 cups fresh bread crumbs

1 cup grated colby cheese

1 tsp dried mixed herbs

1 egg yolk

seasoned all-purpose flour, to coat

oil, for cooking

TO SERVE

bread rolls

slices of fried onion

1 Heat the oil in a pan and cook the prepared onion, mushrooms, and bell pepper until softened.

2 Mash the cannellini beans in a large mixing bowl. Add the onion, mushroom, and bell pepper mixture, and the bread crumbs, cheese, herbs, and egg yolk, and mix together well.

3 Press the mixture together with your fingers and shape into 8 sausages.

4 Roll each sausage in the seasoned flour. Chill for at least 30 minutes.

5 Grill the sausages on a sheet of oiled foil set over medium-hot coals for 15–20 minutes, turning and basting frequently with oil, until golden.

6 Split the bread rolls down the middle and insert a layer of fried onions. Place the sausages in the rolls and serve.

COOK'S TIP

Take care not to break the sausages when turning them over. If you have a hinged rack, oil this and place the sausages inside, turning and oiling frequently. Look out for racks that are specially designed for grilling sausages.

Colorful Kabobs

Brighten up a barbecue grill meal with these colorful vegetable kabobs. They are basted with an aromatic, flavored oil.

NUTRITIONAL INFORMATION

Calories . . . . .131 Sugars 7g
Protein . . . . .2g Fat 11g
Carbohydrate . . . .8g Saturates 2g

15 mins   15 mins

SERVES 4

I N G R E D I E N T S

1 red bell pepper, seeded

1 yellow bell pepper, seeded

1 green bell pepper, seeded

1 small onion

8 cherry tomatoes

100 g/3½ oz wild mushrooms

S E A S O N E D O I L

6 tbsp olive oil

1 garlic clove, crushed

½ tsp mixed dried herbs or
   herbes de Provence

1 Cut the bell peppers into 1-inch/
2.5-cm pieces.

2 Peel the onion and cut it into wedges,
leaving the root end just intact to
help keep the wedges together.

3 Thread the bell pepper pieces, onion wedges, tomatoes, and mushrooms onto skewers, alternating the colors of the bell peppers.

4 To make the seasoned oil, mix together the olive oil, garlic, and mixed herbs or herbes de Provence in a small bowl. Brush the mixture liberally over the kabobs.

5 Grill the kabobs over medium-hot coals for 10–15 minutes, brushing with the seasoned oil and turning the skewers frequently.

6 Transfer the vegetable kabobs onto warmed serving plates. Serve the kabobs immediately, accompanied by a rich walnut sauce (see Cook's Tip, below), if desired.

COOK'S TIP

To make walnut sauce, process 1 cup of walnuts in a food processor to a smooth paste. With the machine running, add ²/₃ cup heavy cream and 1 tablespoon of olive oil. Season to taste with salt and pepper.

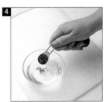  

Garlic Potato Wedges

Serve this tasty potato dish with grilled kabobs, beanburgers, or vegetarian sausages.

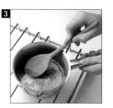

NUTRITIONAL INFORMATION

Calories 257	Sugars 1g
Protein 3g	Fat 16g
Carbohydrate . . .26g	Saturates 5g

🥔 10 mins   ⏲ 30–35 mins

SERVES 4

I N G R E D I E N T S

3 large baking potatoes, scrubbed

4 tbsp olive oil

2 tbsp butter

2 garlic cloves, chopped

1 tbsp chopped fresh rosemary

1 tbsp chopped fresh parsley

1 tbsp chopped fresh thyme

salt and pepper

1 Bring a large pan of water to a boil, add the potatoes, and parboil them for 10 minutes. Drain the potatoes, refresh under cold water, and then drain them again thoroughly.

2 Transfer the potatoes to a cutting board. When cold enough to handle, cut into thick wedges, but do not peel.

3 Heat the oil, butter, and garlic in a small pan. Cook gently until the garlic begins to brown, then remove the pan from the heat.

4 Stir the herbs, and salt and pepper to taste, into the mixture in the pan.

5 Brush the warm garlic and herb mixture generously over the parboiled potato wedges.

6 Grill the potatoes over hot coals for 10–15 minutes, brushing liberally with any of the remaining garlic and herb mixture, or until the potato wedges are just tender.

7 Transfer the garlic potato wedges to a warm serving plate and serve as an appetizer or side dish.

COOK'S TIP

You may find it easier to grill these potatoes in a hinged rack or in a specially designed barbecue grill roasting tray.

Spiced Pilau with Saffron

A Middle-Eastern influence is evident in this fragrant pilau, studded with nuts, fruit, and spices. This rice is ideal served with barbecued lamb.

NUTRITIONAL INFORMATION

Calories	347	Sugars	.........9g
Protein	.........5g	Fat	...........11g
Carbohydrate	...60g	Saturates	.......3g

 2 mins, plus 35 mins infusing/standing 25 mins

SERVES 4–6

INGREDIENTS

large pinch of good-quality saffron threads

1¾ cups boiling water

1 tsp salt

2 tbsp butter

2 tbsp olive oil

1 large onion, very finely chopped

3 tbsp pine nuts

1¾ cups long-grain rice (not basmati)

½ cup golden raisins

6 green cardamom pods, shells lightly cracked

6 cloves

pepper

very finely chopped fresh cilantro or flatleaf parsley, to garnish

1 Toast the saffron threads in a dry skillet over medium heat, stirring, for 2 minutes, until they give off an aroma. Immediately tip out onto a plate.

2 Pour the boiling water into a measuring pitcher, stir in the saffron and salt, and let infuse for 30 minutes.

3 Melt the butter and oil in a skillet over medium-high heat. Add the onion. Cook for about 5 minutes, stirring.

4 Lower the heat, stir the pine nuts into the onions, and continue cooking for 2 minutes, stirring, until the nuts just begin to turn a golden color. Take care not to burn them.

5 Stir in the rice, coating all the grains with oil. Stir for 1 minute, then add the golden raisins, cardamom pods, and cloves. Pour in the saffron-flavored water and bring to a boil. Lower the heat, cover, and simmer for 15 minutes without removing the lid.

6 Remove from the heat and let stand for 5 minutes without uncovering. Remove the lid and check that the rice is tender, the liquid has been absorbed, and the surface has small indentations all over.

7 Fluff up the rice and adjust the seasoning. Stir in the herbs and serve.

Stuffed Apples

When they are wrapped in foil, apples cook to perfection
on a barbecue grill and make a delightful finale to any meal.

NUTRITIONAL INFORMATION

Calories ....294 Sugars 30g
Protein ....3g Fat 18g
Carbohydrate ...31g Saturates 7g

 5 mins   25–30 mins

SERVES 4

I N G R E D I E N T S

4 medium cooking apples

2 tbsp chopped walnuts

2 tbsp ground almonds

2 tbsp light brown sugar

2 tbsp chopped cherries

2 tbsp chopped candied ginger

1 tbsp almond-flavored liqueur (optional)

4 tbsp butter

light cream or thick unsweetened yogurt,
to serve

1 Core the apples and, using a sharp knife, score each one around the middle to prevent the apple skins from splitting during grilling.

2 To make the filling, in a small bowl mix together the walnuts, almonds, sugar, cherries, ginger, and almond-flavored liqueur if using.

3 Spoon the filling mixture into each apple, pushing it down into the hollowed-out core. Mound a little of the filling mixture on top of each apple.

4 Place each apple on a large square of double-thickness foil and generously dot with the butter. Wrap up the foil so that each apple is completely enclosed.

5 Grill the parcels containing the apples over hot coals for 25–30 minutes, or until tender.

6 Transfer the apples to warm individual serving plates. Serve with lashings of whipped light cream or thick unsweetened yogurt.

COOK'S TIP

If the coals are dying down, place the foil parcels directly onto the coals, raking them up around the apples. Cook for 25–30 minutes and serve with the cream or yogurt.

Grilled Bananas

The orange-flavored cream can be prepared in advance but do not make up the banana parcels until just before you need to cook them.

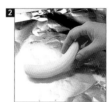

NUTRITIONAL INFORMATION

Calories 380	Sugars 40g
Protein 2g	Fat 18g
Carbohydrate . . .43g	Saturates 11g

🔥 10 mins 🕐 10 mins

SERVES 4

I N G R E D I E N T S

4 bananas

2 passion fruit

4 tbsp orange juice

4 tbsp orange-flavored liqueur

O R A N G E - F L A V O R E D   C R E A M

⅔ cup heavy cream

3 tbsp confectioners' sugar

2 tbsp orange-flavored liqueur

1 To make the orange-flavored cream, pour the heavy cream into a mixing bowl and sprinkle over the confectioners' sugar. Whisk the mixture until it is standing in soft peaks. Carefully fold in the orange-flavored liqueur and chill in the refrigerator until required.

VARIATION

Leave the bananas in their skins for a really quick dessert. Split the banana skins and pop in 1–2 cubes of chocolate. Wrap the bananas in foil and cook for 10–15 minutes, or until the chocolate just melts.

2 Peel the bananas and place each one onto a sheet of foil.

3 Cut the passion fruit in half and squeeze the juice of each half over each banana. Spoon over the orange juice and liqueur.

4 Fold the foil carefully over the top of the bananas so that they are completely enclosed.

5 Place the parcels on a cookie sheet and cook over hot coals for about 10–15 minutes, or until they are just tender (test by inserting a toothpick).

6 Transfer the foil parcels to warm, individual serving plates. Open out the foil parcels and then serve immediately with the orange-flavored cream.